THE SPIRITUAL WHISTLEE
THE BLACK SHEEP SE

MY FAMILY CAN KISS MY ASS

HOW TO DEAL WITH TOXIC, MESSY, NARCISSISTIC FAMILY MEMBERS

CHANEL JASMIN CLARK

Kill Jezebel Media, LLC

PO Box 20486

New York, NY 10009

ISBN – 9798754377868

Printed in the United States

Do you want to book the Spiritual Whistleblower for an interview, speaking engagement or private event?

Please email: ChanelJasmin@gmail.com

CONNECT WITH SWB

IG/TIKTOK: SPIRITUALWHISTLEBLOWER

PATREON: SPIRITUAL WHISTLEBLOWER

TWITTER: ILUVSWB

LINKEDIN: SPIRITUAL WHISTLEBLOWER

CLUBHOUSE: ILUVSWB

YOUTUBE: SPIRITUALWHISTLEBLOWER

EMAIL: CHANELJASMIN@GMAIL.COM

CASHAPP: $CHANELJASMIN

VENMO: CHANELJASMIN

ZELLE: 929-529-3783

PAYPAL: NARCSHITLIST@GMAIL.COM

DEDICATION

I want to dedicate this book to my spiritual family:

Nina, Beth, Brandon,

Pamela, Charoletta,

A. Diamond, Thalan, Beki, Ashley, Nicole, Princess,
Arnold, Toni, Robin, Colby…

(If I have forgotten anyone, please blame my head; you're
still buried deep in my heart).

I love you all.

~SWB

Jesus told them,

"Only in his hometown, among his relatives and in his own house, is a prophet without honor."

~Mark 6:4

Table of Contents

THE SPIRITUAL WHISTLEBLOWER PRESENTS:
THE BLACK SHEEP SERIES VOLUME 1

MY FAMILY CAN KISS MY ASS

HOW TO DEAL WITH TOXIC, MESSY, NARCISSISTIC FAMILY MEMBERS

CHANEL JASMIN CLARK

INTRODUCTION

Wow! I can't believe that I am finally getting around to writing this book about family dysfunction. It's been a long time coming. For the last three years, I've been on a tangent to help people escape toxic relationships through my YouTube videos and nationwide support groups. Just about everyone I can think of, are having relationship problems with a narcissist. During my phone sessions when I'm coaching my clients, I always ask about their childhood upbringing.

Nine times out of ten, what my clients describe to me is narcissistic abuse at the core of their traumas within their families. So many people don't even realize that they were raised by a narcissistic parent (or grandparent). Once I validate and confirm their suspicions about family, their understanding of their codependency issues become clear.

1

We learn toxic-codependency in our youth and it is transferred over into our adulthood. This is why you would attract a narcissist as a lover. Your mother and father programmed you to be addicted to narcissistic energy because they're narcissistic and they "normalized" the toxic behavior in your household when you were a child.

Let me start off by explaining my childhood upbringing. I think that I have been very transparent with my audience. I don't hide my scars. I actually use my life experiences to help people grieve through theirs. I'm not ashamed of anything that I've gone through in life, because all of those bad experiences with every narcissist I have encountered, led me to my God-driven purpose. Once you learn who you are and who God called you to be, everything from your past will make sense. It took me a lot of research and problem-solving to get to the root of my family background to figure out who I was and the direction that God wanted me to take.

I got sick and tired of jumping from one bad relationship to the next. Every time it would fall apart, I would drive myself crazy trying to figure out where I went wrong or how I could fix things. I went into "fixer mode" not realizing that I had been trained as a child, to serve everyone's needs before mine. I mean, that's what a care taker does right? We take care of family. Actually, the term for this behavior is called "**Parentification.**" It's the process where a child/teenager is put into a role reversal position to act like the parent in their household. How many of you had to take care of your siblings because your parents were not around or either too lazy to be the responsible parent that they're supposed to be?

And you wonder why you grew up to become an adult that takes care of other toxic adults before putting your needs first. Look at your parents. They are the ones that programmed you to be a care taker. You cannot fix everyone when you haven't fixed yourself. Your parents don't want you to focus on yourself. They want you to remain codependent and broken (just like they are). If your parents are narcissists, they will want you to take care of them and become dependent on them well into your adult years. They want total control of your money, your relationships, your children and your soul.

Aside from that, let's talk about how your parents programmed you to become toxic-codependent. Before you lose your virginity, your family is already teaching you that your life is of no importance, unless you are married with kids by a certain age. If you notice, the family members who are married for a very long time are usually unhappy with their spouses. Your family would prefer for you to be miserable in a marriage instead of being happy, single and free.

Let me describe my parent's toxic marriage for a bit. My mother was only 19 years old and pregnant with me when she tied the knot with my father. Both of them were too young and too broken to understand what they were both getting into. Some people claimed that my parents were actually in love, but after my own careful analysis, I call bullshit. They were both pressured into marriage by my grandmother (*Nana*) because she wanted to brag to the community that her son (*my father*) was getting married. She also pressured my parents to have grandchildren too (*I was the first grand-child born into the family*). My parents weren't in love. They were two young, immature, controlling narcissists who were entangled with each other, who were governed and controlled by a greater narcissist (*my grandmother*). My father's side of the family had a history of tumultuous, toxic-enmeshed, relationships and my grandmother wanted to carry on tradition by transferring the toxicity down to her sons to further her agenda of maintaining power and control. This was nothing more than a selfish attempt to save face to protect her Jezebel ways and her miserable marriage. All of it was a façade that would later transfer over to her children, grandchildren and great-grandchildren.

My mother already had an established relationship with my grandmother in her late teens because she would do my grandmother's hair after school. It was then that my grandmother (**Nana**) was already playing matchmaker and planning my mother and father's wedding in advance. Hands down, my Nana is a malignant narcissist. She is a very dominant, masculine, controlling, criminal-minded, divisive, mean-spirited narcissist.

Aside from my father, she had two other sons. She completely managed to destroy all of their marriages with her meddling and continuous disrespect of their personal boundaries. Not only that, she would constantly get into arguments and fights with my grandfather (we call him "*Toots*" - may he rest in peace). My Nana was addicted to starting fights; emasculating the men in her family with all of her screaming and yelling. She humiliated her sons all throughout their childhood, causing them all to have long term C-PTSD and anxiety. This toxic behavior was normalized in her household and distributed evenly into her son's lives. My Nana always prided herself on keeping her home spotless and her sons well-dressed, but what took place behind closed doors was a different story.

Dysfunction was the norm in my Nana's household and unfortunately, this was the piss poor example she had set for her sons. Her home wasn't filled with love; it was filled with violence, chaos, destruction and child abuse. It wasn't about love; rather, it was all about the image of looking stable in a miserable marriage. My Nana trained her sons to jump into toxic-codependent relationships so that she may have bragging rights about her sons "appearing" to look stable and happy in their own toxic marriages. Her sons were nothing more than pawns and extensions of her false image and over-inflated ego. It was never about love.

"**Pseudo-Mutuality**" is defined as a structured family system of toxic individuals cohesively bonding together by pretending to be happy whilst fooling the outside community (this is called *Perception Management*). However, they're actually miserable and dysfunctional behind closed doors. All of the abuse and dysfunction that takes place behind closed doors is silenced and swept under the rug. Everyone is taught to never discuss or speak about what takes place in the home, and to always put on a fake smile whenever they leave the premises. Everything all about maintaining a fake image to fool the outside world. This type of family environment livcs within the confinements of their own delusional bubble world.

Whatever takes place in the dark must never be spoken about in the light. This always leaves a traumatic impression on the children.

Toxicity in the family is ignored and normalized. And furthermore, the trauma is taught to the future generation, tainting the babies before they even have a chance to thrive on their own. Toxic family members will even attend church every Sunday to mask the dysfunction. The sermon is never applied at home, so all spirituality and religion is a fake tool to hide the low moral compass of the family's brokenness.

All it will ever be is a facade. Every bit of dysfunction, abuse, deceit, incest, domestic violence, toxic addictions, sexual molestation, fights, gambling, porn, pedophilia and sinful behavior is normalized, ignored and swept under the rug in these types of families. Has any of this ever occurred in your family? If so, please keep reading and remember the term: **Pseudo-Mutuality**.

One thing that I disliked about my Nana's condescending behavior was the fact that she would talk down on me and other women who were single. She would say things like: "*You can't keep a man.*" "*Ain't no man gonna put up with you.*" "*At least I can keep a husband.*"

She would always belittle single women for not being locked down in committed relationships. She would measure and validate herself in comparison to other women, through the lens of her toxic marriage. She thought she was superior to other women who were single because she felt justified in taunting them about the longevity of her miserable marriage.

Her behavior is unacceptable. Training your children and grandchildren to tolerate abuse in their own relationships based on your own horrible marriage is straight bullshit. This is what we call "**Toxic-Codependency**" and it is the root of all of your relationship problems. This is the reason why your family pressures you to jump into a relationship or marriage despite it being toxic and abusive. This is why my parents' marriage was all fucked up. Jumping in head first because my Nana pressured them and paid for a shitty ass shot-gun style, backyard wedding when they had no business getting married in the first place. I digress, my parents were both taught to have weakened boundaries and to seek happiness in each other rather than themselves. My Nana's influence would seal the deal on their marriage and create a generation of domestic violence, trauma, emotional incest, child abuse, drugs, misery, depression and pain. Neither one of my parents had no business getting married that young.

I say all of this to say, that it took me nearly 30 years to figure out my family's trauma and I want to do my part in this world to help bring people closer to God by using my formula to show people the way through my own family history of trauma and abuse. I found that the root of our challenges and issues in life stem from our toxic families. This is what's keeping us separated from God and living a purposeful life.

Our families will try to cripple us if we decide to detach ourselves from their dysfunction. So at the end of the day, they've placed a wedge between you and God whether you realize it or not. We've been conditioned by our loved ones to stay loyal to abuse. With understanding and self-reflection, I pray that you will come to a point in your life where you won't fear cutting off your family permanently. I pray that you will connect the dots to all of your relationships that have failed, and tie them to your parents who initially trained you to attract toxic lovers and bad friendships. From that understanding comes the ability to stop allowing the parasitic host (mom and dad) to feed off of your spiritual energy.

It's time to set your relatives free and regain control of your life. Don't be afraid to set strict boundaries to gain a new sense of freedom. God has so much more in store for you if you would just let go of your past. Forgive your family, but deny them further access. How else are you going to learn to be happy in your solitude if you don't detach from family? I know it's a scary space to be in. Nobody wants to be alone, but that's the solution to your healing. Isolation is where the introspective shadow work takes place. This is where you hold yourself accountable and start the process of expunging your toxic traits that you accumulated by being around your toxic family. Stop prolonging it and do the work.

Don't worry about the financial struggles. It's never easy when you're trying to escape the grasp of your controlling parents. They make it very difficult to leave. If they are helping you pay bills or babysit your children, they will threaten to take all of that away from you in order to cripple and destabilize you. Our parents are our ORIGINAL enemies. Your abuse began with them and transferred over into your love life and friendships. Let go and let God step in. All you got to do is surrender to Him and push your family out. There's a brand new life waiting for you. Let go.

CHAPTER 1

ARE YOU A BLACK SHEEP?

You're reading this book for a reason. Something inside of your brain clicked when you read the title (*and chuckled at the illustration, lol*) right before you made your purchase on Amazon. You want answers as to why you can't get shit right with your family. You can't understand why you are constantly targeted to be the topic of discussion for gossip. Every time you attend a family event, you can feel the negative energy when you walk into a room and you get a sense of anxiety knowing that you will be gossiped about once you leave the room. Are you tripping? Family can't be that bad right? We're supposed to constantly forgive family no matter how many times they do us wrong, I suppose. Or at least that's what society pressures us to do.

All of your life, you always knew something was wrong. Not only were you bullied in your household, but you had to face bullying in school. What was wrong with your parents back then? They never seemed to validate your traumatic experiences in school. They didn't seem to care about your accomplishments or you making the cheerleading squad. It just feels weird. Growing up in a family where you never develop an identity of your own destroys your self-esteem. They rob you of your childhood for their own selfish gain.

You're constantly teased by family. Your personal achievements are ignored or discredited. Your childhood is stripped from you because you are pressured to take care of your siblings and work a part-time job to help support your family. This forces you to grow up too fast. This can't be life right? You want to know why you were targeted, shamed and left to feel like an outcast in your own family. It's because you're the **Scapegoat Child**, better known as, "*The Black Sheep.*"

A "**Scapegoat Child**" is the one sibling that is singled out and punished relentlessly by the narcissistic parent(s) for wrongdoings and the smallest mistakes. You are usually berated in front of other family members. The beatings and verbal abuse are over-the-top compared to your other siblings. Everything you do and say is magnified and used against you. You have now become the whipping post of the family. There are two types of Black Sheep and I will break it down to help you determine which category you fall in.

The *"Good" Black Sheep*. You are more likely to be this one because you're an **Empath**. Despite all of the abuse you suffer, you are constantly bending over backwards to take care of your family. You have a heart of gold and they take advantage of your kindness and generosity. Your parents don't protect you from bullies or abusive people in general. They allow your siblings to disrespect you. Yet you still continue to forgive them over and over. You are a beautiful soul crying out for someone to love you and support you because your trifling family depletes your spirit.

The *"Bad" Black Sheep*. If you happen to fall into this category, then you are more than likely a toxic-codependent or narcissist. The bad black sheep is criminal-minded and doesn't give a shit about hurting his/her family. They will continue to misbehave and dish out the same disrespect that they receive from toxic family members. The bad black sheep is a rebel and he will latch on to the dysfunction of the family. He has a "love/hate" relationship with his toxic parents and won't disconnect from them.

You're more than likely the good black sheep and I can tell you now that you have been selected by God to be the "*Chosen One*" of your family. I wholeheartedly believe that when you were conceived in your mother's womb, God marked you to take on the greatest task of breaking your family's generational curse. Yes, even before you were born, God marked you. It is an honor and privilege to be selected by God to carry out such a difficult task. He was being very selective when He chose you. This is why your family attacks you the way that they do. They see the anointing and they hate that you were chosen to receive it.

If you can remember the story of Moses from the book of Exodus, his story is no different than yours. He suffered at the hands of the Egyptians (*his adoptive family*). They saw Moses' anointing, but refused to acknowledge it. It wasn't until the power of God was unleashed through Moses, that everyone saw the power of God Almighty. It's always fun to bully the **Black Sheep/ Scapegoat Child**, until God steps in to deal with the evildoers.

I know it gets draining to deal with family, but please keep going. Stand your ground. Stop allowing them to get away with bullying you. Stay away from family events; you're not obligated to go. Stay away from places they hang out and don't associate with anyone connected to them. Your family wants you to believe that you can't exist without being dependent on them. They want you to stay connected to their toxicity so that they can continue to gossip about you and boss you around. You are the **Scapegoat** remember? They have assigned you the position of being the **Black Sheep** for their sick, sadistic pleasure to dismantle your self-esteem and everything beautiful that God created you to be. They are jealous and competitive of the natural gift that was bestowed upon you by the Almighty. It's not your fault.

Holding the title of the **Black Sheep** won't be easy growing up. Your family will bully you and then you will then go to school and be bullied by your classmates some more. Believe it or not, being raised in this toxic environment, you will also attract toxic friendships and relationships that resemble the same abusive behavioral traits as your family members. This is why you continuously attract narcissists into your life. Look at your family and the bad treatment they have dished out all throughout your childhood. You were being groomed to receive bad treatment from the world and you weren't even aware of it.

I want you to wear your **Black Sheep** badge with pride. Your family is just mad that their attempts to berate you and destroy you have continued to backfire over the years. Once you become an adult, they will seek to stay enmeshed with you to control and strong arm you. If you find your way out and start to live an independent life, you will be ridiculed for maintaining your distance from them. This is the life of the **Black Sheep**. Once you find your power, you need to give them your ass to kiss and there won't be anything that they can do about it!

Let me help you find your power… It's right there inside of you and has been all along. Your family doesn't want you to tap into your powerful anointing, but it's a new day. I'm gonna show you how to tap in, and remind you that you are loved by Jesus, no matter how poorly your family treats you. The good Lord did not create you in His image to be mistreated by anyone; not even family.

So buckle up your seat belt and get ready for my **Black Sheep** boot camp. By the time you finish reading this book, you will feel empowered to set boundaries with your trifling family and start living your life on your terms! Fuck them people. They've done enough damage to your life and now it's time to reclaim your peace, your joy and blessings! Tell your family to kiss your ass and don't look back! God saw how they treated you, so you're not obligated to worry about them anymore. Go on and live your life!

The **Black Sheep** always turns out to be the "**GOAT**" (*The Greatest of All Time*). God is waiting on you on the other side of your healing journey. Cut that trauma bond and release your family so that you can get what's rightfully yours. Just because your family members are broken and dysfunctional, doesn't mean that you have to spend the rest of your life tolerating it.

CHAPTER 2

NARCISSISTIC ABUSE IN YOUR FAMILY

So you see the word "Narcissist" plastered everywhere all over social media. It has become the trending topic amongst relationship gurus and life coaches all over the internet. People are driven to do a Google search on the symptoms of NPD and end up exploring millions of YouTube videos and blogs that define narcissistic abuse. Everyone wants to throw the word "*narcissist*" around very loosely without having the in-depth knowledge of what narcissism truly entails. Just because someone is toxic, doesn't necessarily mean that he/she is a narcissist. We all have toxic traits that we must evolve and grow through. It's really important that you can distinguish the difference between full blown NPD versus having narcissistic traits.

The difference is that a narcissist lacks accountability to do so. A narcissist doesn't want to grow, he can't. He is a hamster on a hamster wheel going nowhere fast. His disorder is what feeds his ego, so he self-sabotages and constantly repeats his cycle of abuse with every victim he preys on.

The real question is, why aren't our doctors, school teachers, therapists, pastors, political leaders and lawmakers not teaching us about this particular form of covert emotional abuse, as well as how to identify it in people? Our children should be learning about this in school.

Why aren't they teaching narcissistic abuse to prepare our teens for the real world? I will tell you why. It's because this information cannot be taught if we come from a narcissistic society and a government that enables this behavior to go on without severe consequences. There is pressure to constantly forgive abusive family members. We are forced to work alongside narcissists in a toxic workplace environment where we have to tolerate covert abuse in order to receive a paycheck.

Even the church excuses abuse (*Which is why a lot of children are molested in the pulpit by bishops and pastors, I digress*). We are living in a world with a system that sets us up to fail because narcissistic abuse is not recognized as domestic violence or abuse at all. Yet it is the root to everything that disrupts and destroys humanity and animals.

How can you identify the narcissists in your own family, when you don't have the education or awareness to spot the early signs? Well that's my job. I'm gonna do my best to help you. A lot of people have a misunderstanding of what healthy parenting looks like, so let's debunk the bullshit.

Narcissistic Personality Disorder is both genetic and environmental. It is a personality disorder that is taught by an abusive individual, usually a guardian or caregiver, and passed down to a child, hindering the emotional development of that said child. The child then grows up to be an adult with an emotional void due to the abuse he/she was exposed to in their childhood. Instead of the narcissist taking steps to correct the toxic behavior that he was taught in his childhood, he will proceed to go on in life and repeat the abuse he suffered. He will use those same abuse tactics towards his friends, family and romantic partners. He basically repeats the abuse cycle that was taught to him in his adolescent years.

A **narcissist** is a person who lacks empathy, remorse and accountability of his mistakes. He is detached from reality and he basically creates his own reality with the help of the people who are always nearby in proximity (*his toxic enablers*). A narcissist is a highly manipulative, insecure, competitive, jealous, envious, greedy, destructive backstabbing demon. Narcissists are energy vampires and they are always on a constant quest to latch on to people who secretly admire them, yet seek to destroy the very same people due to their own jealousy. They have no purpose or identity, so they steal and copy from others. All of their friendships and relationships are transactional.

Although they are horrible human beings, they manage to reel people in with their forced charm and wittiness. They are charismatic and talented in every way. People are drawn to them like a moth to a flame. Narcissists love to prey on

Empaths with codependency issues and they are driven by money. They have an excessive need to take other people's money (*even if it means to scam*) and even steal from their children.

The narcissist needs fuel to sustain his lifestyle. This energy source (*emotional reaction*) that he steals from his victims is called **Narcissistic Supply**. If you cannot be used in any capacity, whether it is your money, time, resources, sex or being there at their beck and call, you will be discarded like trash. The narcissist can only survive if he or she has a group of toxic enablers supporting his bad behavior.

The narcissist is a pathological liar, troublemaker, demon-possessed thief of joy. They love drama and destroy anyone who seeks to live a peaceful life. In the end, they lose many friendships and lovers because they refuse to address their sadistic, egregious behavior. Their bad karma follows them like a dark cloud looming over their pathetic life. They constantly make poor choices because they fail to change their devious and deplorable behavior. They have absolutely no remorse or empathy for the way that they hurt others.

Narcissists abuse their targeted victims in a cycle of three components: **Lovebombing**, **Devaluation** and **Discard**. They are passive aggressive in their approach to secure their victims which can be tedious in itself. This is why it is very common for them to turn their own children into victims automatically. Children are seen as objects and pawns. A narcissist doesn't love his/her children, he merely uses his children to trap and manipulate more victims to add to his harem of supply.

The **Lovebombing** Phase is where the narcissist treats you like a priority. It is during this time that you are made to feel special and loved. The predator moves fast to sweep you off of your feet, flooding you with compliments, buying you unnecessary gifts and showering you with affection. This whirlwind romanticizing is usually very swift as the narcissist needs to move fast to destabilize you. He can't do that until he is able to get you to drop your guard to allow him access to your heart. **Lovebombing** is also carried out in toxic friendships and relationships.

The **Devaluation** Phase is when the narcissist feels that you have lowered your guard enough so that he can start to dismantle your self-esteem. It is during this time that the underhanded insults begin. You will be gossiped about, laughed at, mocked and triangulated (*we will discuss Triangulation later on in the book*). You will feel as if you are in a competition that you didn't ask to be in. The narcissist is slowly but methodically chipping away at your soul, molding you into the perfect doormat to be used at his personal discretion. You are being trained like a puppy and rewarded with crumbs. Those crumbs are bits of attention that the narcissist deliberately deprives from you when he dishes out the silent treatment when he feels like the relationship is becoming boring.

Another tactic is **Gaslighting**; a nasty manipulation tactic that causes one to doubt their own intuition and reality. The narcissist will constantly poke and provoke you to have an emotional outburst, using lies, stonewalling, strategic deflection and dismissal of whatever problem you bring to them. You will be invalidated and mocked if you dare hold the narcissist accountable or call him out for his bad behavior. You will be punished infinitely.

The final stage of the abuse cycle is the **Discard Phase**. This is the most brutal part of the entire process because the narcissist doesn't give a shit about how much pain he is causing you. He enjoys your suffering and has put together a nasty smear campaign riddled with lies, rumors and excessive put downs. He wants you to beg and plead for him to go back to the nice guy that he once was in the beginning of the **Lovebombing Phase**, but you're gonna learn that it was only a representation of his false self. The person you fell in love with in the very beginning, never existed. You are discarded like trash while the narcissist flaunts his new favorite person in your face. He will also assemble a group of friends and family to help him spread the smear campaign. Once he feels he has broken you, he will leave you alone and return at a later date to restart the entire abuse cycle all over again.

So now that we've got that out of the way, can you identify anyone in your family who acts like this? Seriously, when was the last time that you actually analyzed all of the personalities of your family members? Just because you didn't see any traces of physical abuse, doesn't mean that you weren't abused. Matter of fact, I'm going to break down the different forms of abuse that you may have been exposed to as a child and then you can make a determination which one of your parents or grandparents are narcissistic.

Covert narcissists are the trickiest of them all because they know how to come off extremely empathetic. They can be gentle but very unresponsive and detached from their children. They also have a habit of hiding amongst the church congregation every Sunday. They are the main churchgoers who abuse their loved ones Monday through Saturday, and repent on Sunday, just to start the abusive cycle all over again on Monday. Church is a cover up for their insidious, closeted behavior. Coverts are silent, but deadly and they usually can get away with more abuse and make it look effortless.

Overt narcissists are more outspoken than coverts. Their outlandishness brings them narcissistic supply and attention in various ways. These are the types of narcissists that deliberately cause a scene to gain attention. Their bold "*in-your-face*" approach is what entices them to elicit an emotional reaction out of you. Immoral, loud, incredibly arrogant, boisterous and delusional. They incite fist fights and arguments, but they're usually the weakest one in the room. They don't mind letting people know that they are attention whores because they don't care. They're also very destructive and physically abusive towards people and animals.

So the question remains: how do you identify this behavior in your parents, siblings and grandparents? Well let's discuss. If your parent(s) were great at providing for you financially, but they never seemed to offer any emotional support, then they could very well be narcissists. When you become an adult, your parents will continue to use money and/or gifts to control you or your siblings, and even your children. A huge misconception that people have a hard time grasping is that financial support is a form of love. I'm here to tell you, that it's not. Buying your affection is used as a means to control you.

Financial Abuse is an abuse tactic used by narcissists to exert control over their victims. Although money is a huge factor in providing the bare necessities that a child needs in order to grow and develop, emotional nurturing is more important. Your parents could raise you in a beautiful home and they could very well have their college degrees and good jobs. However, if they are emotionally disconnected from you, and all they ever do is buy you things and pay your bills, then this is a form of narcissism. They are controlling you financially because they do not know how to love you properly. They could care less about giving you hugs and kisses, all that matters is that the control stays in-tact. You will also notice that your parent(s) spoil your siblings more than you, which is also a form of financial abuse because they are using their monetary power to divide you and your siblings.

Narcissists use money and gifts to control their victims. It starts with spoiling a child with toys and money to train the child to stay up under the narcissist's wing. The narcissist creates a trauma bond by giving gifts and rewarding bad behavior with more gifts. This will train the child to become clingy, self-entitled and narcissistic. This method is guaranteed to create a monster with self-entitlement issues.

The narcissist will spoil one child and punish the other child by taking away the gifts in front of the other children. This is how long-term sibling rivalries are initiated. When you become an adult, your narcissistic parent will continue to spoil your adult sibling. They will either be able to live off of your parents with little to no rent payment, get their car note paid or any other bill. So even as an adult, your parents are controlling your siblings with money. The moment you decide to move out and become independent, your parents will discard you, while continuing to spoil your adult sibling. They also view their grandchildren as pawns. If you reject the money and gifts, you will be discarded like trash and your narcissistic sibling will reap all of the benefits.

Let's just say that you get an SSI check, but you still live at home with your narcissistic parents, they will take your check from you and spend it on themselves. This is another form of **Financial Abuse.** I've heard all types of stories where the parent(s) stole tax refunds from their children, lawsuit money, college loan refunds, foster care checks, you name it. And if you are still living with your parents as an adult, they will want you to pay rent and take care of them. If you make any mention of moving out, they will cripple you and destabilize your efforts to move out. The goal is to keep you stuck at home where they can consume your money, time and energy for themselves. Your money is their coveted money in their sick, twisted minds. If you have children, they will want to take custody of your kids and sue you for child support. They don't give a shit about your children, but they will use them as pawns to suck money from you. Even babysitting money. Narcissistic parents are money-hungry savages.

If one or both of your parents are narcissists, then there's a great chance that your grandparents are as well. It's time for you to dig into your family history and get some answers about their behaviors. This may be hard to do, because like

I said earlier, narcissists love to do their dirt and sweep it underneath the rug and deny that it ever happened.

If your parents weren't around to raise you or either worked excessive hours throughout the week, this is **Abandonment/ Emotional Neglect.** Being absent from a child's life deprives him of the emotional connection that he needs to develop effectively in order to process his own emotions. Narcissists will dump their children on other family members to raise them while they run the streets and/or start a whole new family elsewhere. So ask yourself, which one of your parents were absent during your childhood and didn't care? **Emotional Neglect** is in fact, narcissistic abuse.

Last but not least, let's talk about the most difficult one: physical, verbal and sexual abuse. Many of us was molested and beaten badly throughout our childhood. More so, we are the targeted child out of our siblings and we are punished more than the other children. For some strange reason, your narcissistic parents chose to pick on you more than your siblings. Your beatings are more severe. The name-calling is brutal. The sexual assault is repetitive. The family is aware that you are being abused, but they don't care or won't step in to put a stop to it. You feel alienated and scared to speak up. You don't understand what you ever did wrong to deserve such torturous, sadistic abuse. It's almost as if your parent(s) enjoy putting welts, bruises and markings all over your body. They enjoyed touching your body parts and lying on you to make you look like a fool. I'm so sorry that you had to endure this. I've walked in those shoes and I absolutely despised my family members for treating me like an outcast, knowing that I had been molested and beaten badly.

Now is the time to learn about narcissistic abuse in depth. It's bigger than your romantic relationships or the fake friendships you've had get to get rid of in the past. This is the core of who you are and why you make such poor choices in the people you invite into your life. This isn't the time to be dating or jumping into a new relationship. It is now a time to self-reflect, isolate and detox. Your spirit needs expunging of the toxicity it has consumed over the years.

This requires you to be celibate and laser-focused on recovery. If you come from a family of narcissists, you are going to have to fight like hell to get rid of them forever.

CHAPTER 3
TRIANGULATION

Triangulation is the narcissist's most used manipulation tactic where he will "pit" you against a third party in the most calculated way. This third party can be one individual, or either a group of people. The narcissist will proceed to turn this third party against you while trying to turn you against them. Whether it's a friendship, relationship, kinship or total stranger, the narcissist will have everyone fighting against each other while he sits back and enjoys his popcorn. It doesn't matter if you are aware of whom the third party is or not, the narcissist has set you up in a very dangerous situation that could potentially land someone in the hospital, jail or worse.

The whole point of **Triangulation** is to create a volatile atmosphere where everyone is fighting over the narcissist. He has mastered the art of playing puppet master to multiple parties by staging a cat fight and sitting back to enjoy the show. This attention brings him an enormous amount of narcissistic supply. **Triangulation** also allows the narcissist to feel in control of everyone involved in the altercation. It is a power move to dominate and manipulate everyone's emotions for his own personal gain to stroke his over-inflated ego.

If you notice that your parent(s) gossip about you to your siblings and vice-versa, then they are deliberately keeping their children at odds. Not to mention, they want you and your siblings to be jealous of each other and competitive. **Triangulation** allows your parent(s) to play you against your siblings while creating insecurities in both of you. It's a very devious way to destroy a child's self-esteem. So please reminisce and think back to your childhood. Did your parents ever make you feel less than your siblings? Does your sibling continue to gossip about you behind your back with your mom or dad? I want you to realize that this behavior was taught by your parents. **Triangulation** is narcissistic abuse. Here are some examples of Triangulation within your family (*see the illustrations below*):

Example #1

Parents vs. You vs. Your Siblings

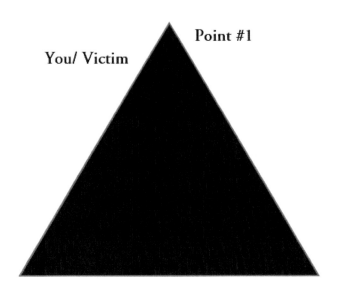

Point #1
You/ Victim

Point #2
Parent/ Abuser

Point #3
Siblings

Example #1 – In this scenario, your parents are constantly putting you against your siblings. This creates jealousy, competition and insecurities amongst all of you in order to appease your parent's ego. Your parents enjoy seeing their children fight and tattle tale on each other. It makes the narcissistic parent feel in control to have each child report back what was said. None of the children realize that it is the narcissistic parent that started the fight to begin with. It's basically the narcissist playing puppet master over his children and inciting fights to feel in control.

The behavior continues into adulthood because the narcissist's need to control his children becomes obsessive. Now that you're an adult, your parents will continue to use **Triangulation** against you and your siblings to keep you constantly pulled into the family drama. You will have to cut off both parents and your siblings in order to put an end to this incestuous love triangle. Your parents will continue it for as long as they can get away with it if you don't put your foot down. They love to see their children fighting. No normal parent would want their kids at odds with each other. Only a narcissist would provoke their own children to harm one another.

Example #2

Parents vs. You vs. Your Family Members

Point #1
You/ Victim

Point #2
Parent/ Abuser

Point #3
Family

Example #2 – In this scenario, your parents and siblings will gossip about you to other family members. For example, if you confide in your narcissistic father that you dislike your cousin, your father will then turn around and discuss everything you told him about your cousin, to other family members so that the word can get back to your cousin.

Your father deliberately went against your wishes to keep your secret and now your cousin is angry at you. If your siblings are narcissistic, they will spill all of your secrets to other family members to build a secret alliance against you. They will speculate about how much money you make and your lifestyle and your children. They will manage to get your family members to jump on the bandwagon to dislike you. Your family will also connect with your enemies to form an alliance against you. This is **Triangulation**.

Example #3

Parents vs. You vs. Your Lover/ Spouse

Point #1
You/ Victim

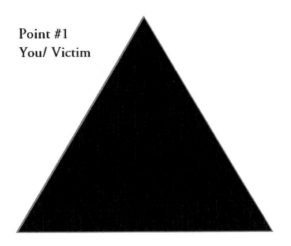

Point #2
Parent/ Abuser

Point #3
Lover/ Spouse

Example #3 – This might be the nastiest of them all. When you are involved romantically with a narcissist and you're going through a nasty breakup or divorce, your family will team up with your lover to come against you. You have to realize that your parents have set you up to fail in life. The person you are in a relationship with is basically a reincarnated version of your narcissistic mother and father.

Your family knows that your relationship will fail and they anticipate you running back home to get away from your abuser. They will regain control over you if you do move back in with them once your relationships fails. However, if you do not return home to your narcissistic parents, they will form an alliance with your toxic lover and they will all team up against you to gangstalk and cripple you. Your family's betrayal is unreal. They should be protecting you from your abusive lover, yet they're making excuses and overlooking the abuse that you received from your toxic relationship. They will also help your lover destroy you in family court. This is all **Triangulation**.

Example #4

Parents vs. You vs. Your Friends

Point #1
You/ Victim

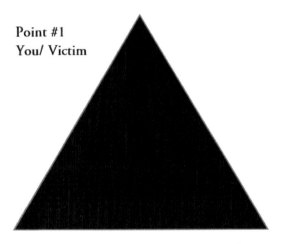

Point #2
Parent/ Abuser

Point #3
Lover/ Spouse

Example #4 – If your parents do not like your friends or if they feel that your friends will pull you away from them and help you level up, your parents will seek to destroy your friendship. They feel that your friend is a threat to the control that they have over you, so they seek to drive a wedge in your friendship to break it up. If your friends happen to be narcissists, then you parents will bond more with them.

When you decide to cut your parents off, they will reach out to all of your old toxic friends to form an alliance. Your parents will bond with your enemies in an attempt to keep tabs on you. They will have your old friends stalking your Facebook and reporting back. The goal is to turn everyone connected to you (*former friends and exes*) against you. Your parents are punishing you for breaking free from their control. This is a form of **Triangulation**.

CHAPTER 4

BLOOD ON THEIR HANDS

One of the most common things that I hear Empaths complain about in their childhood is being molested by a family member and being ignored for exposing it. I mean family is supposed to protect you from things like this right? So why aren't they? Do you know how it feels to be a young adolescent who is forced to walk on eggshells and interact with his/her predator while the family pretends not to see it? I dealt with this pain for many years and I'm very disappointed at my family.

I talk about my experience all of the time, but I will go into detail here. When I was about 13 or 14 years old, I was molested by my mother's second husband (*I refuse to call him stepfather*). My mother being a full-blown narcissist, married this horrible man immediately after divorcing my father. She wasted no time locking down her drug-dealer, pedophile hubby. It was all about the money, because he is an unattractive man. My mother is a gold digger, so she hit jackpot when she met him. But as karma works its magic, he ended up in prison and lost all of his money running behind my mother.

Allegedly, my mother went off to prison for about 4-5 months. My family told me and my siblings that she was going away to some diet camp (*all lies*). I guess she was too embarrassed to tell her children the truth, so she had family lie to us. I was the oldest of three children. Once my mother went away to serve her time, arrangements for who would babysit me and my siblings were put in place. From Monday through Friday, me and my siblings would stay at my Nana's house (*where my trifling father was living at the time*), and they took care of us. On the weekends, they sent us to go stay with the pedophile.

I remember it like it was yesterday. My Nana gave me a pretty peach-colored chiffon night gown. Our house wasn't very big, so our beds were all in one bedroom. My siblings were in the bunk bed, and I slept in a twin bed adjacent to them. Sometimes me and my brother would switch from bunk to the twin bed, but my younger sister always slept on the top bunk.

One night, I wore the night gown and I could feel the pedophile's hands fondling my ass! He startled me out of my sleep. At that moment, I stopped breathing. I froze up. I could hear him breathing on me. He didn't know that he woke me up, but he kept his hands on my ass. My heart started pounding and I was terrified. At that split second, all I could do was pretend to wake up and move around (*this was enough for him to back off and get scared once he realized I was waking up*).

I was scared and I had no one to turn to. I had a reputation in the family for being soft-spoken, and very shy. I wasn't the one to speak up for myself. My mother always called me horrible names and made fat jokes about my weight and size. If I dare speak up for myself, she would become violent. I was beaten severely most of my childhood, so I was silenced. I was programmed to take on the abuse and to never speak up for myself. I couldn't get up the nerve to tell my father and grandmother. Who would believe me?

The pedophile continued to tip toe into our bedroom every weekend and touch me on my ass. He knew that I would never be able to tell anyone, or rather, nobody would believe me. Besides, the pedophile was a drug dealer with a lot of money. He gave my family money and they kissed his ass for more. Even if I had shown them any evidence, he had them eating out of the palm of his hands because he gave them money. He had my family in his back pocket while my mother was away. There was no one for me to run to or confide in. I don't understand what would possess him to take my innocence away from me. I still have nightmares about it to this day. I don't wish this mental anguish on anyone.

When my mother was finally released from prison, she came home and resumed her evil behavior. Prison hadn't humbled her or taught her anything. We ended up having to pack up and move to South Carolina because the pedophile was facing criminal charges for smuggling and distributing drugs. Once we got to South Carolina, my mother turned up the abuse and the pedophile ended up going away to prison. It was at that time that I confessed and told my mother what he had done to me while he was locked up.

I'm not sure if my mother talked to my father about this, but she did tell my toxic, enabling grandparents about it. She totally shunned me away and swept everything underneath the rug. It was almost as if she was angry at me for exposing her predatory, pedophile husband. What's sickening is that he already had a known history for being the town player.

He slept with one of my mother's close girlfriends. She was ready to fight the woman, however, when it came to her own child, she completely dismissed me and stayed married to this horrible man. I mean, he's not even my biological father. My mother failed as a guardian and protector. She was supposed to follow through with a police report and open up an investigation with Child Protective Services. Nope. She stood by her pedophile husband and is still married to him right now.

By the time I reached my senior year in high school, there was an incident where my mother had taken a curling iron and struck me in the face right next to my eye. She left a nasty open gash on my face. I felt so embarrassed walking around the school hallways with the nasty wound. My mother marked my face so that my classmates could laugh at me.

Well God must have been looking out for me because my Guidance Counselor pulled me to the side and asked me what happened to my face. I was terrified to tell her, but she could kind of sense that something bad happened to me at home. She called me into her office to talk about it. I confessed everything to her because I was sick of my mother treating me like shit. I told her about the verbal, physical and emotional abuse. I also told her that I had been molested by my mother's pedophile husband. It was my last opportunity to tell someone other than family. I was desperate to be heard because my mother refused to believe me.

My Guidance Counselor proceeded to call Richland County Department of Social Services and report my mother and her pedophile husband for child abuse and sexual assault. Of course I was scared because I knew my mother would throw a nasty fit when the social worker got in contact with her. Her narcissistic rage went through the roof when she found out she was being investigated. I ended up running away from home at the end of my senior year of high school to go live with my best friend. The investigation stayed open for a year and was found inconclusive because the pedophile was all the way up north locked up in prison and they could not complete their assessment or investigation of what he had done to me. I also left home to go to college in Louisiana. I had turned 18 years old which made me an adult. So they closed the case.

I still had no closure all of these years and I have had nightmares of the sexual molestation, replaying over and over in my head. My mother and father failed me. My family members failed me. How do you learn about a child being molested within your own family and turn the other way? How can you sleep at night? My mother's close girlfriends knew about the abuse, yet they still remain enablers of her toxic behavior. I could never be friends with a woman who abuses her children or enables her children to interact with a pedophile. I have lost so much respect for my mother's girlfriends. I guess that's why they say "birds of a feather flock together. They're all toxic-codependents.

I say all of this to say that I can feel your pain. If anything like this has ever happened to you and your family turned their backs or either protected the abuser, then they all have blood on their hands. The **Scapegoat** child will always be bullied, silenced and made to look like a liar with mental issues. I endured all of this.

This is why I do not deal with any of my immediate family members or any of the family that enables my mother and father's irreprehensible behavior. A child should feel protected by his/her parents at all times. I have a daughter and I would kill anyone over her. Sometimes I'm a bit too overprotective of my daughter, but I always want her to know that I got her back.

You have to cut your family off when they pretend not to see the dysfunction, abuse, pedophilia, infidelity and all other forms of toxicity in the family. They know it's there, but they "*sweep it under the rug.*" They will invalidate your pain and suffering and continue to interact with your abuser. They will invite your pedophile uncle to Thanksgiving dinner knowing it makes you uncomfortable. The elders don't want to hear about any sexual molestation and will even defend the abuser. And if you try to stay away from family functions for this very same reason, they will make you feel guilty for distancing yourself. It's a no-win situation.

I will encourage you to change your phone number and do not give it to any of your family. I would also encourage you to deactivate your Facebook page and relocate to another city/state. Get away from these toxic enablers. They see the abuse, but they will never acknowledge it. At the end of the day, God saw everything and He will be your vindicator against your parents and the predator who took advantage of you.

I want to conclude by telling you, no matter your decision; you do have the power to file civil and criminal charges against the predator. These days, lawmakers are extending the statute of limitations for victims of sexual crimes to come forward and file charges against their abusers. I would encourage you to do the same. Times are changing and more people are putting their abusers on blast with lawsuits (*and winning*).

Your family is wrong for protecting the abuser, but I want you to know that they will all be dealt with accordingly by God. Whether or not you choose to forgive your parents or the individual who molested you, is a personal choice. I don't pressure people to forgive their abuser. That's a decision you have to make and it involves consulting with God. I don't think the good Lord will penalize you for not being able to forgive, so don't let society or your toxic family pressure you into forgiving your abuser. Your childhood was robbed from you. Take your time with healing and forgiveness. Stay far away from toxic family and work on becoming a better person so that you don't repeat your family's toxic behaviors and pass them down to your children.

CHAPTER 5

KEEP THEM OUT OF YOUR BUSINESS

I think the title of this chapter is self-explanatory. When I coach my clients, I have to constantly drill it into their heads to keep all of their personal business to themselves. Too many of yall run your mouth to your family members and then you get mad when they turn around and gossip about you. **Keep your family out of your business!**

Let's just say that you fall on hard times. You might have gotten laid off from your job or you were involved in a car accident that left your vehicle stuck in the shop for six weeks. Why would you tell your toxic family members and expect them to be sympathetic about your downfall? Misery loves company and they will be laughing at your problems behind your back. You better get into the habit of keeping your private life to yourself. Don't even confide in one family member. Don't trust any of them. It might sound cruel, but you're better off safe than sorry. **Keep your family out of your business!**

If you have children and they're having behavioral problems in school or their grades aren't good, do not tell anyone in your family. Protect your children because your toxic relatives love to embarrass and exploit anything that could potentially hurt you. When people gossip about kids, it's hurtful and you better believe your family will talk about yours. **Keep your family out of your business!**

Another thing, if your child happens to be developmentally-delayed or have any disorders such as Autism, ADHD (Attention Deficit Hyperactive Disorder) or ODD (Oppositional Defiant Disorder), please spare giving your family the details of the treatment. When you come from a family full of narcissists, they will discourage you from placing your children in therapy for behavioral problems or disorders. Narcissists believe that children are easy targets to groom, molest and manipulate. If a child doesn't receive proper treatment or therapy for their issues, then the narcissists in your family will attempt to mold your children into future narcissists, turning them against you. Trust me, you don't want those problems. **Keep your family out of your business!**

Narcissistic people are deeply insecure and very unhappy with their own lives. They do not care to hear about the joy in other's lives because it will piss them off.

CHAPTER 6

HOOVERING

When you finally decide to cut off your family, they will all come together to do what is called **Hoovering**. Now what exactly is **Hoovering**? Well if you remember the **Hoover** vacuum cleaner, then you'll have a sense of what the word means. Whether it be a friendship, relationship or family matter, once you break free from a narcissist and go **No-Contact**, they will cyber stalk you and try to get in touch with you to get you to break **No-Contact**. Don't do it!

Your family will become real aggressive with breaking your boundaries. Just like a vacuum cleaner, they will attempt to *"suck you back in"* to the family dysfunction just to punish you all over again. Remember, you are the **Scapegoat**. If you escape, they will have to find someone new to bully. That's why they're obsessed over your absence and will make multiple attempts to get in contact with you. You have to be vigilant when making them respect your boundaries even if it means calling the police on their nosey asses.

Your family will pull together to **Gangstalk** you. What exactly is **Gangstalking?** It's a collaborative effort by a group of miserable people to stalk you via means of social media, phone calls, text messages and even popping up in person (*driving past your house and uninvited house visits*). Your toxic parents will recruit family members to monitor you and pass messages back and forth to get you to break **No-Contact.** Please don't do it!

I remember when I cut my mother off many years ago and I was still on Facebook. I didn't realize that she had several relatives stalking my Facebook page. I received friend requests from distant cousins and inbox messages from aunts that I haven't seen in ages. They were contacting me to try to "guilt" me into contacting my mother. They totally disregarded my boundaries or the fact that I can't stand my mother and wanted nothing to do with her. My family is fully aware that I was beaten severely by mother throughout my childhood and molested by her second husband. They know I don't want any contact with her, yet and still those motherfuckers disregard my boundaries. I blocked every last one of those bastards to send the subliminal message back to my mother that she needs to leave me alone. I don't give a fuck if her house was on fire or whether she was laid up in the hospital with pneumonia. Leave me the fuck alone! Period.

I cut my mother off well over 10 years ago, and she continues to stalk my social media pages. She's fully aware that I am a huge social media influencer with a growing international fan base. She knows that I can't stand her and I absolutely want nothing to do with her, yet she obsessively stalks me from a fake page. All of her attempts to send her messengers *(they're referred to as '**Flying Monkeys**)* have failed. She is fully aware that if she sends anyone to contact me, I won't respond other than blocking that said individual. Thanks to her, the damage is already done. After my repeated attempts to mend our broken relationship multiple times, I have contended with the fact that our relationship will never work due to her dysfunctional and abusive behavior. The fact that I have family members who refuse to hold her accountable and will actually aide her with covering her tracks knowing she abused me, is insane!

No matter which one of your parents are narcissistic, just remember that the stalking doesn't end. It will continue five years from now... even twenty years from now. The obsession to regain control over your life, your children and your finances is scary. They hate to see you thriving and successful. They hate to learn that you are being a better parent to your child then what they were to you. They hate to see you earning your college degree and making good money. The mere fact that they can't control you or any of your blessings makes them green with envy. The plan was never for you to escape the household and level up. It was always meant for you to fail. That's how sick your parents are.

When they can't get you to break **No-Contact** because you are hip to their manipulation tactics, they will recruit other family members to contact you to make you feel guilty for detaching from their poisonous grasp. Please don't fall for this bullshit. It's all a game. If you go back, the abuse will resume and they will hurt you ten times worse than what they did the last time. Don't be a fool. Narcissists enjoy placing you on a pedestal just to kick you off it to watch you fall on your face. They are sadistically enjoying your fall from grace. Remember, you are the **Scapegoat** and "*emotional punching bag*" of the family. If you return after being abused, they will rejoice in knowing that they got their doormat to come back again for another round of abuse. Aren't you tired of running on the hamster wheel of hell? The definition of "**insanity**" is to keep doing the same thing over and over again, but getting the same results. Let that sink in before you decide to break **No-Contact**. Forgive them, but stay far away from them and enjoy your newfound peace.

CHAPTER 7

SMEAR CAMPAIGNS

One of the most hurtful things that I have ever had to endure was hearing both of my parents gossip and spread lies about me to other family members and peers. Every time I thought I was confiding in them, they would turn around and tell all of my secrets and personal business to others. Both of my parents also kept me and my siblings divided up by putting us against each other. What's even worse, is hearing my parents gossip and smear each other. I felt like I was in the middle of an ongoing war. I mean they literally still smear each other to this day, and it has been over 30 years since their divorce.

This is where I found through my own research, that narcissists are notorious for obsessing over their victims and spreading nasty smear campaigns once you escape them. This includes toxic friendships and relationships as well.

Narcissists all operate from the same playbook, no matter what the environment. Once you flee from their grip, you will have to endure a monstrous, hateful smear campaign riddled with lies, rumors and negative gossip about you. It's painful, but I'm here to help you push through it.

Why would a family member start a nasty smear campaign about you? What sort of validation do they get from gathering a group of people together to annihilate your reputation? Well, like I said before, the narcissist's job is to keep you crippled, isolated and dependent on them at all times. They want to control your life. They are jealous of your pets, your children and your friends. Anything that jeopardizes their control over you, will be placed on the radar to be destroyed. If you're reading this book, you have already cut off your family permanently, or you're either contemplating it. Wherever you are in your healing process, please brace yourself because your character will be destroyed by your relatives once you leave the nest.

Your independence is a threat to their entire existence. If you're anything like me, then you have already been suffering nasty smear campaigns all of your childhood. This is actually more sadistic because when you're a child, you literally have to depend on your family for everything and you can't run away from the abuse. They will gossip about you in your face knowing you can't hide from it. I was always teased for being obese. My parents always had something negative to say about my weight. I can remember my father saying, *"You'd be so much prettier without all of that weight."* Or my mother repeatedly telling me, *"Look how big your thighs are, you fat bitch!"*

Both of my parents would then talk about me to others. The crazy shit is they both destroyed my self-esteem and then criticized me for getting into relationships with abusive men. There was zero accountability for their contributing to my lack of self-worth because they all played a part in annihilating it. How do you destroy your child's self-esteem, then turn around and criticize her for attracting abusive men to fill the void for the lack of love you never gave her? Make it make sense!

Then what's worse is that your parents will train your siblings to be narcissistic. Whether you have a brother or sister, they will too jump in on the smear campaign per your parent's orders to abuse you further (*this is called* **Abuse by Proxy** *or* **Third-Party Abuse**). Your siblings will continue to help your parents gossip about you once you become an adult. It doesn't end. They will constantly spy and pry to have something to talk about when it comes to you. Your income, friendships, car, house, relationships, hobbies and everything in your life, will be placed under a microscope and gossiped about on a regular basis. These people do not have a life.

When you finally move out of your parent's house and cut off family, the smear campaign will intensify because you seized their control over you. The smear campaign is all that they have left. It makes them feel in control to sit up and gossip about you because they feel that if they are able to control other people's perception of you, then it will still make them feel in control after you have detached from them. This is really sick and twisted. The extent that your family will go to in order to destroy you because you cut ties from them is baffling.

As hurtful as it may seem, please ignore the smear campaign. Do not engage in any damage control. Do not contact family members to clear your name. Do not post subliminals to your family on social media. Matter of fact, you need to deactivate your Facebook until you are fully healed. The smear campaign will reveal every single enemy in your family. Whoever continues to stay connected to your abusive parents, must be cut off. I don't care if it's your grandparents, cousins or whoever... They all must be blocked. Change your phone number and call **911** if they trespass your home. Invest in a Ring Video Camera Doorbell.

Let them talk all of the shit they want. Let them speculate and make up rumors. Just as long as they don't intrude or violate your personal boundaries, they can run their mouths as long as they stay on their side of the fence. Your job is to keep leveling up and being successful. Your achievements and accolades will make them all look dumb.

Silence is always the best answer to toxic family members spreading a nasty smear campaign. Give them your ass to kiss!

CHAPTER 8

ELEVATION REQUIRES SEPARATION

When you're the **Black Sheep** of the family, you will work hard to achieve your parent's validation. What usually ends up happening is that your narcissistic mom and dad will be emotionally-detached. You will receive little to no support or acknowledgement for your achievements during your adolescent years. The only time your parents will ever brag about you, is to make themselves look good (*especially on Facebook*). You have to remember that narcissists view their children as extensions of themselves. They live vicariously through their children and claim their children's achievements as their own, stealing credit from the child.

Because they have no identity, they will steal their child's identity and envy it at the same time.

They will never acknowledge you as an individual with your own identity; however, they will be the first in line to claim the credit from the success of your hard work to make themselves look good. They want to gain **narcissistic supply** from the attention you will receive from your wins. Yet, the fucked up part about this is that they will also be low key jealous of you at the same time. You have to remember that narcissistic parents are in constant competition to outshine their own children. The jealousy is very real.

I remember wanting my mom's validation so much that I would bend over backwards to please her. She was never satisfied with anything I did. When I was a senior in high school, I worked 2 jobs and my mother stayed home on her fat ass watching soap operas. Every week that I would get paid, she would snatch my entire pay check to take care of the groceries and bills. She refused to get a job. At the same time, she was abusing me and making sure I never left the house.

I had become her personal slave until I left for college in Louisiana. When I received my acceptance letter for college in the mail, she was quick to get on the phone and brag to other family members that I had been accepted to an all-black college. The flip side was, she was also jealous and mad that I would be moving out and taking away her control over my money.

You will burn yourself out trying to please an ungrateful, narcissistic parent. The more you work hard for their validation, the more hoops they will make you jump through. You might as well wear a red clown nose and put on a wig. They are training you to perform for them like a circus clown with no reward insight. You will turn into an over-achiever yearning for the love and acceptance of an emotionally-void parent. You're never gonna get it.

One other thing I want to point out is that your narcissistic parents will never give you the life skills in order to make it on your own. They never teach you about taxes, buying a house, paying bills, personal hygiene, etc. The reason that they refuse to teach you these important skills, is because they want you to remain "*child-like*" and easy to control. If you get a backbone and gain some independent life skills, you won't need the help of your parents anymore.

They fear that your independence will threaten their control over you. They want you to fail at life so that you can run back home to them for more punishment. It's really sickening when you realize how miserable they are and how their misery will affect your life if you don't distance yourself. It is imperative that you isolate yourself after you have detached from your toxic family.

Nobody said it would be easy. Yes, you're gonna feel guilty. Yes, you're gonna miss them. Yes, you're gonna get the urge to pick up the phone and call them. Yes, you're gonna miss them on holidays. However, you must separate from them if you are going to heal properly from being the **Scapegoat** of the family. You can't stay in touch with any family members, no matter how nice they appear to be. Your healing depends on the strength of your newfound boundaries. It will feel lonely for a while, but what grows from it will be phenomenal.

You will be on the right path to healing when you separate yourself from your original abusers: mom and dad. If your siblings are narcissistic, you cannot talk to them either. Your parents will use your siblings against you to keep tabs on you. Everyone must be blocked. Don't play with it or you will suffer the consequences. Once you isolate, you can begin your therapy sessions to treat your toxic codependency issues, as well as your PTSD. It is in your isolation period that you learn how to reinforce your boundaries and stop tolerating disrespect. This is the lonely part, but if you push through it, you will never want to deal with your toxic relatives ever again, because you'll be too addicted to the peace and tranquility that you have gained through separation. Don't be scared, just do it and never look back. You got this!

CHAPTER 9

HOLIDAYS & VACATIONS

One thing is for certain, two things are for sure, narcissists are extra petty when they don't get their way. They walk around harboring and projecting so much misery, that they deliberately destroy holidays and special events for their loved ones. Whether it's your birthday or graduation, Thanksgiving or Christmas, the narcissist will find a way to cut deep to ruin your special day. If you pay close attention, you will notice a pattern of passive-aggressive behaviors before, during and after the special holiday. What's the strategy behind all of this? Why would someone go out of their way to destroy your birthday or not even acknowledge you during the holidays?

When the narcissist can no longer control you emotionally or financially, he/she will discard you like trash and pretend that you don't exist. The crazy part is, while they're pretending to make you disappear from their life, they're actually stalking you and keeping tabs the entire time in the midst of their silence. The silent treatment is meant to punish you for not complying with the narcissist's warped rules and regulations. The narcissist hates the fact that you're independent and free from their toxicity. So, it's apparent that he deliberately chooses the holidays and any special event, to torture you by ignoring your existence.

Treating you like shit during a holiday brings the narcissist sadistic joy. The narcissist knows that you are naturally empathetic and family-oriented. They know that holiday time is special to you. The narcissist doesn't care, just as long as you're aware that he deliberately ignored you during your special day. Your birthday will be erased from his calendar. He will either ignore your invite to your college graduation or sit in the audience and not clap for you when your name is called to receive your diploma. They ruin special moments.

If the narcissist has grandchildren and you refuse to allow the narcissist to control you, they will ignore their grandchildren's birthday and discard the child like trash. Grandchildren are also pawn pieces to the toxic narcissist. They are disposable if the narcissist cannot exert his power over you. Do not allow the narcissistic grandparent to treat your child like crap. It's okay to not allow your children to visit their abusive grandparents during Christmas. It's okay to reject the fake gifts. It's never from the heart anyway.

Do not feel guilty if you choose not to visit your relatives during special holidays. If you are depressed about it, don't sit around the house drinking your life away. Get up and get dressed. Call up some friends and go out to eat. Volunteer at a soup kitchen and help the homeless. Do something nice for someone less fortunate. If you don't have any friends, then it's okay to treat yourself to a movie and dinner. Go ice skating or take a painting class. The goal is to stay busy to keep your mind off of your toxic relatives and exes from past relationships. I know the holidays can be a hard time, but you will need to maintain your boundaries and learn to be happy on your own. That's how you break the trauma bond and codependency cord.

Mother's Day and **Father's Day** are very difficult holidays for those who were raised by abusive parents. Many struggle with contacting their guardians and may feel guilty in not doing so. Let me just remind you that the bible scripture **Psalm 27:10** states, "*When your mother and father forsake you, the Lord will take good care of you.*" Why would you feel guilty for not contacting them when they have been treating you like shit all of your life?

If you think being loyal to abuse is helping you overcome your childhood trauma, then think again. Staying loyal to toxic relatives is pure stupidity. It's actually **Toxic-Codependency.** The Lord loves you and He doesn't want your parents to abuse you. Say a prayer for them and leave them alone on the holidays. You mirror their behavior right back to them, ignore them and find something fun to do to and enjoy your day. They will abuse you even on holidays, so tread carefully.

Last but not least, I strongly recommend avoiding going on vacations with your toxic family. They will ruin your trip. Narcissists are notorious for ruining vacations. Go with a friend or go by yourself, but don't bring your relatives. Your entire vacation will be placed under a microscope, closely monitored and gossiped about. You will be judged for simply having a good time!

Vacations are just that. A time to get away from all of the stress in your life and enjoy a new environment that's calming to your soul. Why would you bring along a toxic family member? All they will ever do is sneak and take unattractive photos of you with their cell phone to show to the rest of your family. They will talk about how much money you spent buying souvenirs. They will also feel entitled for you to pay for everything. Why put yourself through the added aggravation? Do not bring family on your trip. The idea of taking a vacation is to alleviate stress, not create more for yourself.

CHAPTER 10

STAY AWAY FROM FAMILY FUNCTIONS

Now that we've got the holidays covered, let's discuss family functions. As you continue to distance yourself from your toxic relatives, you will be pressured to attend family events. Weddings, Baby Showers, Family Reunions, Christenings, Get-Togethers, Barbecues, Dance Recitals, you name it. Let me tell you something, don't go. It's a trap and I will tell you why.

Whenever toxic family come together for an event, it is grounds for a "*set up*" to make fun of the **Scapegoat** of the family. How can I put this rather? It's a premeditated way, to lure you into the fire to kick you down on the ground. Family events are an opportunity for toxic relatives to dig into your personal business; throwing jabs at the same time.

You will notice small groups of relatives gossiping and giggling amongst each other as you walk into the room. You can just feel the negative energy. You grab a seat and sit quietly only to listen in on them gossip about everyone in the family and their mama. Your stomach has knots in it because you don't feel comfortable entertaining gossip and you know the moment that you get up to leave the room, they're gonna start talking shit about you.

When you are raised in a narcissistic family, every family gathering will be full of gossip sessions and drama. The family will tell you it's all love when in reality, it's all mess. You know damn well your relatives are messy as fuck. They can't wait to start asking you who you're currently fucking. Why are you single? Where's your baby daddy? How much money do you make? Where do you currently work? How big is your house? What kind of car do you drive? How did you afford the nice things that you have? Why don't you have kids yet? When are you getting married? Why do you take so many vacations? Why don't you spend more time with family? Where's your ex and why didn't he come along with you? Nosey motherfuckers.

You see, it's never really about being around your loved ones and enjoying each other's company, it's really about everyone showing their true colors and feeling safe in a toxic environment to justify it. The bullshit will be tolerated and allowed at your family's gatherings. It would be strange if nobody gossiped or did anything out of the norm.

Your perverted crack-head uncle is watching all of his nieces walk around. Your messy ass cousins are gonna go in the next room to smoke some weed and gossip about what everyone is wearing. Your aunts are sipping wine and bringing up old dirt against each other from 50 years ago. Your drunk granddaddy starts cussing out his brothers in front of everybody. Nobody is safe.

Piece of advice, if you don't feel like being bothered, don't go. Stop allowing your family to dictate your emotions by making you feel guilty. Take charge of your life and reinforce your boundaries. You are not obligated to attend any family events. God will not punish you for turning your family away. Peace is priceless and your energy must be preserved. You can't afford to be surrounded by a bunch of energy vampires and spiritual parasites looking to deplete your time.

They will use every opportunity to dig into your personal life, ask rude questions and make false assumptions. They will feel justified in doing so because they know that they have you outnumbered. Don't go. Throw your own events with your friends and enjoy the peace that comes with it. If your family has a problem with it, block them. They should be blocked anyway from reaching your phone. Don't even allow them access to invite you to anything. Problem solved.

CHAPTER 11

HEALTH ISSUES & FUNERALS

S o, it's human nature for the elderly in your family to become sick or disabled. If your family is anything like mine, there's a history of diabetes, breast cancer, kidney disease and high blood pressure that runs through my bloodline. Even your parents may fall sick and you will receive a phone call one day that they're in the hospital. People struggle with wanting to reach out to help their family members whenever someone falls ill. How do you handle this if you are practicing **No-Contact** as well as reinforcing your boundaries?

You kindly mail a card sending well wishes for a speedy recovery. That's enough to acknowledge the family member who's ill while maintaining your distance. This also sends the message that your boundaries are very much in-tact and you intend to stay in your safe space to maintain them. When you handle things in a mature manner, your family members can't attack you. Of course, they will attempt to make you feel guilty for not visiting your family member in person while he/she was in the hospital, but that's none of your concern. You're grown and as an adult, you can do what you want. Nobody can "*strong-arm*" you into doing something that you don't want to do. Let family be mad. Let family talk their shit. Let them gossip. The bottom line is, you were considerate enough to acknowledge the family with a thoughtful card and prayer for a speedy recovery. You don't owe them anything else.

See me personally, I wouldn't send no damn card. I wouldn't send shit. And if I happen to fall sick, I wouldn't want them to send me shit either. I don't want no toxic motherfucker praying over me while I'm sick in the hospital and shut in. I honestly don't believe that narcissistic people are children of God. I believe they serve Satan, so their prayers and well wishes would be coming from a dark place and I would not heal properly due to their black magic and false prayers. Fuck them people. Stop allowing them to make you feel guilty because you've chosen to live a peaceful life.

You gotta remember, narcissists are great actors. One of the ways that they attempt to reel their victims back in, is by using their illness to make you feel bad for leaving them. A lot of narcissists will even fake their illnesses hoping you'll get scared and break **No-Contact** to check up on them in the hospital. Don't do it. If you have one solid family member who isn't toxic, you can use them as a person of reference to keep up to date with emergency family matters (***I wouldn't do it, but I'm not going to discourage you from doing it***). You already know who the sane family members are. Everyone else can go to hell.

Now let's discuss funerals. This is a tough one. I mean, I've been in this situation and I can explain it from two different perspectives. Over the last nine years, I have lost three family members. I lost my paternal uncle in 2013, and I lost my maternal grandmother in 2015. My uncle was only 49 years old when he passed away peacefully in his sleep. I received a call from a relative and I was in utter disbelief. He was so young and his death was not expected. He was an avid community activist and leader. The local fire department, police force and mayor all attended his funeral. I normally don't attend funerals, but I had to make an exception for my uncle because I was his favorite niece.

At the time, I was not speaking to my mother. I had cut her off previously a few years prior for her toxic behavior. I knew I would see her at my uncle's funeral and it was a risk I was willing to take to be the bigger person. I didn't know what narcissistic abuse was at the time, so I continued to forgive my mother whilst giving her the benefit of the doubt. Every time I would run back and try to mend our relationship, it was the same shit. She is the most passive-aggressive, delusional, jealous-hearted, competitive basket case I have ever encountered in my life.

I show up to my uncle's funeral and my mother walks in with my grandmother. I was standing there with my daughter and I walked up to my mother and attempted to hug her. She was wearing dark sunglasses and was very cold. Her body language was very stand-offish. So, let's see, you haven't seen your daughter or granddaughter in several years and this is the behavior you display at a funeral where family is supposed to act civil to each other?

Her behavior was repulsive. Even at the burial and repast, she wouldn't look at me or hold a conversation. She refused to sit down and eat with me at the reception. I've never seen a woman who was more jealous and threatened by her own daughter. Her true colors came out at the funeral, but I handled it all with class. I didn't allow her to run me out of the place. I stayed, ate my food and had a nice time talking to distant relatives. I took pictures and then I left. I haven't seen or spoken to my mother since the funeral.

Like I said, it's been nearly nine years and she's mad that I don't chase her or beg her for shit. I'm independent, make my own money and I don't allow her to control my daughter. She hates that she can't control me and her behavior reflected that at the funeral. She couldn't even act like a mother during a time of vulnerability. I'm ashamed to call her my mother, but that's how narcissistic mothers treat their daughters when they are extremely jealous. Cold and callous. God have mercy on her soul.

Now what I have learned from that experience was that I don't belong around toxic family members. My mother wasn't the only narcissist at that funeral. There are many family members who enable her disrespectful behavior towards me, knowing damn well that she's abusive and evil. I know who these specific family members are, and I had to cut them off too.

When my maternal grandmother passed away in 2015, I didn't attend the funeral. I had learned my lesson from attending my uncle's funeral. I wasn't going to allow my mother to disrespect me ever again at a family function. I felt sorry that her mother died, however, I was not going to risk any chances of her being a covert bully towards me at my grandmother's funeral. I sat this one out.

What I did instead was purchase a big bouquet of flowers with my name and my daughter's name written across the banner and I had them delivered to the funeral home. It was a nice gesture to let my family know that I was there in spirit even though I had chosen not to attend. It also sent an indirect message to my mother, that I don't want to be in her presence and that I was not going to tolerate her blatant disrespect this time around.

Look, what I'm trying to say to you is this, funerals are nothing more than a platform for toxic family members to bully and gossip about you. The person that has died, is dead and gone. That individual doesn't care whether or not you show up to the funeral or not. You only feel pressured to attend because you're more worried about what your family members are gonna say about you if you don't attend. Fuck them people.

Guess what? They're gonna treat you like shit if you do decide to attend. Send some flowers, card and money and stay home. Maintain your sanity. Once the dust settles, allow a few months to go by and go visit the cemetery. Bring some flowers and make peace with the deceased. You will have your opportunity to pray and say your last words in the presence of God without any distractions or family drama.

Whatever you do, make sure you do it to please God and not your toxic family. That's all that matters.

My grandfather recently passed away in 2020 during the Thanksgiving holiday and I did not attend, nor do I feel bad for not attending. I understand my power. I understand that my family's toxicity and dysfunction won't change simply because someone died. I realize that I am a moving target. I am the **Scapegoat** of the family and I know that my family would seize any moment to pull me back in to initiate the abuse cycle all over again, yes, even at a funeral.

My advice, don't attend funerals. Send flowers or a card. Visit the cemetery at a later date and make peace. Don't set yourself up to be emotionally abused by family ever again. God won't judge you if you choose not to attend. He knows your heart.

CHAPTER 12

COERCIVE ENMESHMENT

I will keep this chapter short and to the point. You know what's really fucked up? When you're trying to move on with your life and your stalking ass family members decide to make **911** phone calls and false police reports or mental wellness checks to intrude your personal space.

They will lie and tell the police that you're having a mental break down. They will instruct the police to show up to your front doorstep to do a mental wellness check. When you open the door and see the police, you're totally thrown off guard. Why did the family send the police to your house to perform an unwarranted, fake check-up?

If you have children, your toxic ass mama will go to drastic measures to ruin your life when you don't allow her to control you. She will resort to calling Child Protective Services on you because she's envious of your relationship with your child. She knows that she wasn't a good mother to you, so she will go out of her way to try to destroy your good reputation as a mother. She will even tell her friends that you're are a bad mother.

My mother called CPS on me and filed a fake report to try to get me in trouble. Each time that I was investigated, my case was closed in less than two weeks because the social worker could not find any traces of abuse. They would interview my daughter's school teachers and I always received high raves about being a good parent. Not to mention, my daughter attended a specialized school for disabled children, and she had four teachers to one class room due to her special needs. These teachers and pediatric therapists were trained to see early signs of abuse in children. If I were abusing my daughter, her teachers would be the first to report it to CPS before my mother could get a chance. See God don't like ugly. Every time my mother tried to make prank calls, it would always backfire.

Another thing that my narcissistic mother did to try to regain control of me was file a fake police report stating that she felt threatened for her life. She lied on her police report and told them that she lived alone when in fact, she had been living with her pedophile husband for over 35 years. She was trying to make herself look like a damsel in distress. She stalks my YouTube channel every day and she got mad that I stated my disdain for her in one of my old Mother's Day videos.

I stated in my video that I would cause harm to her "should" she ever attempt to violate me and my daughter's personal boundaries. I was speaking in terms of self-defense. I never made a direct threat towards her. She then utilized that video to try to get a permanent restraining order against me. The judge rejected it, because it wasn't a direct threat nor have I stepped foot in that wench's house in over 20 years. She knows damn well that I pose no threat to her. I avoid family functions because I don't want to be in the same room with her. She was trying to force her way back into my life!

She was hoping to obtain a permanent restraining order because she would have made more fake phone calls to the police to have me locked up. We don't even live in the same state, but this bitch wants to find any reason to bully her way back into my life. She knows that I don't want shit to do with her. I don't want her money or her time. I want her to disappear forever.

Let me explain, the last three examples I just gave you are forms of **Coercive Enmeshment**. It is a form of manipulation that the narcissist will use to bully his way back into your life by getting you to break **No-Contact**. It's a forced way for them to get you to interact with them when they know you don't want shit to do with them. It's really sick.

All I can say is to keep a paper trail of all receipts to prove your whereabouts. Do not stay in touch with family members because they will turn on you and help your abuser build a case against you.

They will try to get you into the courtroom to gain custody of your children even. They will use the courtroom as a means to bully you too. This is called **Vexatious Litigation**. The bully tactics are never-ending when you decide to escape. Stay diligent and keep a record of documents for evidence to cover your tail. If they continue to violate your boundaries through **Coercive Enmeshment**, you can file charges against them for **Vexatious Litigation**.

Know your rights and stop allowing them to disrespect your boundaries! Protect yourself and protect your children or else they will turn your children against you and have you sitting in jail or either a psych ward!

CHAPTER 13

THERAPY

Once you cut off your family and begin your journey to healing, you will have to seek out therapy at some point. I want to caution you about a few things before you dive into your therapy sessions. When you are looking for a good therapist or psychiatrist, you want to make sure you find the right one. Your job at this point, is to cut ties with family, isolate and seek out intensive psycho-therapy. Please be very selective when choosing a therapist. You want to choose someone who is familiar with narcissistic abuse, domestic violence, child abuse, incest, rape and PTSD. You want to make sure that you feel validated in your sessions and comfortable with sharing intricate details of your childhood.

Not to scare you, but there are many doctors and therapists who are narcissists themselves. That is very dangerous to sit there and vent your problems to another demonic evil doer. Just imagine telling all of your pain and misery to someone who has absolutely no empathy for humans? How can he/she even possibly help you heal? Narcissistic therapists and doctors are scammers. They only care about gaslighting you so that you can keep returning back for more sessions. It's all about the money. Not your healing process. You want to make sure that you research the best quality care. You want a professional who is spiritual, empathetic and thorough. Be careful who you vent your problems to. They will string you along and throw word salad at you. Many of my clients have told me that they have not gained much from therapy with their therapists because they didn't feel that the therapist understood narcissistic abuse. Well if the therapist is a narcissist, he/she will become triggered during your session, causing him/her to reflect on their own behavior while they help you sort through yours. Let that marinate!

I went to many therapy sessions over the years, however, I did my own research on narcissistic abuse and came to the conclusion that my mother and her pedophile husband are both criminal-minded sociopaths. They both have an "above-the-law" mentality and feel that they both can commit crimes and get away with it (which is why their marriage has lasted so long because they both enable each other's bullshit).

Stay out of the church too. The church is full of narcissistic predators. Society has pressured us to run to church for our problems only to be met by a harem of pedophiles, closeted homosexuals/ lesbians, polygamists and predators. Your family will force you to use church in place of actual therapy knowing church is toxic as hell and won't help you heal. Yes you're supposed to pray when you have problems, but therapy is what works. Your process won't begin until you cut all ties to every single last toxic individual in your life. Choose your therapist wisely.

CHAPTER 14

SUNDAY SERMON

In the last chapter, I spoke about narcissists teaching you (the **Scapegoat**) to use church as a means of "therapy" to replace actual therapy. When you grow up in a toxic environment surrounded by narcissists, you will come to realize that they don't want to fix their dysfunction. They constantly repeat the trauma and keep it within the family. What they will do is run to church every Sunday after they have committed all types of sins throughout the week. They believe that they can save face and deflect their demonic side by attending church every week. **Narcissists are Fake Christians.**

A lot of my clients are born into toxic, covert religious families where their fathers are pastors. Let me tell you something, the pastors and ministers are the worse types of narcissists. Every Sunday the pastor has his entire family sitting in the front pew along with the first lady (his wife). His kids are dressed beautifully and his wife is decked out with her brim hat and silky pantsuit with matching rhinestones. His family "appears" to be well put together. Little do people know that the pastor is abusing his family behind closed doors. That's because the pastor is a covert narcissist hiding behind the pulpit. He abuses the name of the good Lord to "mask" his insidious abusive behavior.

Between society and our toxic family pressuring us to run to church when we are going through hard times, we aren't even cognizant that we are being set up to sit in the congregation amongst a bunch of wolves in sheep's clothing. The church is by far the most toxic place to go if you want to heal. There are very few churches that genuinely help people (*from a spiritual and moral standpoint*). Sure these fake churches will be seen handing out turkeys to the community during Thanksgiving or holding fundraisers to help the less fortunate. All of that is about façade. But what goes on behind closed doors is another story. Most of these narcissistic pastors are pedophiles, adulterers, woman-beaters, thieves and predators, hiding behind a veil of Christianity.

When your narcissistic parents force you to go to church with them, they are doing it for the wrong reasons. They think that by going to church every Sunday, it will make the family and outsiders view them in a positive light. Your parents don't want the world knowing that they are abusing you when nobody is looking. Church helps them conceal their deception. Once church is over, your parents will go back to being abusive throughout the rest of the week. They are spiritually-disconnected from God because they continue their abuse as if He is not in the room while they're doing it to you. How delusional. Our Father above can see everything. Narcissists make a mockery out of God and they continue to traumatize their children in spite of God watching them. The bible has scripture that protects us from abusive parents. Don't let your parents fool you into believing that you must constantly "*honor*" them simply because the bible says so. Again, this is what we call "**Toxic-Codependency.**" Yes, the good Lord wants us to honor our parents, however, He also wants our parents to respect us just the same. When you have narcissistic parents, the respect is never reciprocated because your toxic parents have low self-esteem. They're too busy trying to compete with their own child out of pure jealousy.

Listen, I grew up in a Baptist church. I didn't find out until later that my mother (*allegedly*) had slept with the pastor of the church. She was a teenager at the time, and she led the church choir. Our pastor was a pedophile, yet my mother continued to attend his church while forcing me and my siblings to attend as well. The rest of the week, my mother was verbally and physically beating the crap out of me and my brother. I couldn't understand how she could sit up in church pretending to be a saint, and then abuse her children Monday through Saturday. How inconsistent! But this is the life of a narcissist. They have no integrity or moral compass. Everything that they do is to protect their false image. I realize now that my mother was never a woman of God. She used the church to uphold her façade and still does. She ain't fooling God though. That's why I stay far away from her, because she has deluded herself that she won't receive any karma for abusing her children and allowing her pedophile husband to get away with molesting me. She will have to pay for all of the pain and suffering she has caused her children. I don't want to be near her when that karma hit.

Please raise your discernment and stop trusting the church. You don't need a middle man to find God. We have been tricked into believing that church is the only outlet to seek healing (in replacement of actual therapy). That is not true. The church is full of narcissistic predators, starting with the pastor on down to the finance committee. I don't give a fuck who gets mad. I said what I said. I don't look pastors the same anymore. They are full of hidden scandals waiting to be exposed.

If you want to find God, you can turn your own home into a peaceful sanctuary. Stop attending church with your toxic family members. Matter of fact; don't even attend the same church as your relatives. You always have the option to worship online from the comforts of your home. Bless your house. Do a spiritual cleansing and mop the floors with ammonia. Anoint your doorways with olive oil. Line your home with sea salt for protection. Burn your Sage or Palo Santo. Burn your white candles for protection and purification of toxic energy. Store a bowl of lemons in each room to absorb toxic energies lingering in the air. Keep protection crystals by your bedside. Spray your walls with Florida water. Pray. Pray. Pray! Ask God to protect you at all times from demonic family members. Ask Him to keep you and your children shielded from all enemies and anyone wanted to destroy your peace. Church is not what it seems. It's a place where vulnerable and innocent people are preyed on. Stay out of the fire and build your own relationship with God. Trust me, He doesn't care how you choose to worship Him, just as long as you stay connected to Him every day. Don't let family guilt you into going to church. It's a set up.

CONCLUSION

I t's not easy to break away from toxic family members. I've spent the last 30 years trying to get this thing right. So many nights I have cried because I wanted to attend family gatherings, but I knew I had to stay away in order to keep my sanity. It's not easy. You are an Empath and your love is genuine. You still love them, even after they have torn your reputation to shreds. You still love them, even after they never supported your endeavors. You love them, even though they never showed up to your college graduation. That's the tough part about being an Empath. We tend to love people, even after they have done us wrong.

Listen, I used to hate being the **Scapegoat**, but now I actually love it. You wanna know why? It's because I figured out that it is an honor and privilege to carry such a title. Being the **Black Sheep** is actually a wonderful badge to uphold because it ain't for the weak. You are in fact appointed to be the Moses in your family. The assignment is to break the generational curse within your family without any instructions.

Just as Moses had gotten sick and tired of the way that Pharaoh treated the Israelites, he went against his adopted family and their laws because he knew that they weren't in alignment with what God wanted. There was something special inside of Moses to be a natural leader and curse-breaker. He had what we call "*Purpose*" and so do you!

God had called Moses to step into his assignment to go free the slaves. It wasn't an easy task and yes Moses had to flee his family or else they would have crippled him and killed him. He would end up in the wilderness, hungry, cold, isolated and in fear. There were moments where Moses thought he would starve and die in the middle of nowhere, but what he came to realize was that God was with him all along.

This is what you have to realize. The reason why your family bullied you all of your life, is because God marked you to break the generational curse. You just didn't know that you were "chosen" for the assignment. That's why the numerous attacks came. Now you're here reading this book because you are ready to answer your calling. It's time for you to claim your spot and do your work on behalf of God, just as Moses did.

The generational curse ends with you and the legacy you decide to leave behind. Once your relationship with God intensifies, you will be at peace with your life. You won't feel guilty for cutting off your family or blocking toxic people at all. You will actually remove people from your space without blinking. It gets easier over time.

So go in peace and step into your purpose if you already haven't done so. Help somebody in need, who's fighting to get away from an abusive relationship or friendship. By helping others, you're actually doing the work as a prophet of God.

When you look back at everything you have endured, you won't regret any of it. Those bad times built you up to be who you are today. I definitely wouldn't change a thing about my past. It turned me into Super Woman and I now look forward to destroying narcissists. My discernment is sky high. I feel invincible and blessed. Ready to go to war for the good Lord. Everyone can't wear that badge of honor. It holds too much power.

So congratulations, you are on your way to spiritual freedom and inner peace. When you understand that you're not obligated to honor anyone except God, your whole perspective on life will change. I pray for you and your healing process. Don't give up; it's wonderful on the other side of the rainbow. You're one fabulous Black Sheep and you better own it! ~SWB

ABOUT THE AUTHOR

Chanel Jasmin Clark is a certified Life Coach and Narcissistic Abuse expert. In 2009, Clark received the honorary Susan B. Anthony Award from the National Organization for Women (NOW) for her activism in the NYC Fashion Industry. She is also a survivor of narcissistic abuse and has managed to turn her pain into purpose for the sake of helping others escape emotionally-abusive relationships. She has now devoted her time to conducting national tours to hold support group meetings for victims of domestic violence.

Clark began her educational and media studies at HBCU, Grambling State University. She transferred to New York City and later completed her Bachelor's Degree in Mass Communications at SUNY Empire State College, and a Master's degree in Media Management at the Metropolitan College of New York. She is now pursuing a Doctorates in Psychology.

In 2022, she will continue to travel internationally to expand her support groups around the world. Her primary agenda is to utilize her platform to bring awareness about Narcissistic Personality Disorder to help individuals identify the signs of covert, predatory behavior in the initial stages of meeting people.

THE SPIRITUAL WHISTLEBLOWER PRESENTS:
THE BLACK SHEEP SERIES VOLUME 1

MY FAMILY CAN KISS MY ASS

HOW TO DEAL WITH TOXIC, MESSY, NARCISSISTIC FAMILY MEMBERS

CHANEL JASMIN CLARK

Printed in Great Britain
by Amazon